3 9082 0975 5504

D0983166

My Big Backyard

Javelinas

Lola M. Schaefer

Heinemann Library
Chicago, Illinois

Customer Service 888-454-2279
Visit our website at www.heinemannlibrary.com

Designed by Kim Kovalick, Heinemann Library; Page layout by Que-Net Media
Printed and bound in China by South China Printing Company Limited.
Photo research by Bill Broyles
Edited by Tameika Martin

08 07 06 05 04
10 9 8 7 6 5 4 3 2 1

Library of Congress Cataloging-in-Publication Data
Schaefer, Lola M., 1950-
  Javelinas/ Lola M. Schaefer
      v. cm. – (My big backyard)
Includes bibliographical references (p.   ).
Contents: Are javelinas in your backyard? – What are javelinas? – What do javelinas look like? – How big are javelinas? – What do javelinas feel like? – What do javelinas eat? – What is something special about javelinas? – How do javelinas stay safe?
  ISBN 1-4034-5046-3 (hardcover) – ISBN 1-4034-5734-4 (pbk.)
  1. Collared peccary–Juvenile literature. [1. Collared peccary. 2. Peccaries.] I. Title.
  QL737.U59S36 2004
  599.63'4–dc22
                        2003021019

Acknowledgments
The author and publishers are grateful to the following for permission to reproduce copyright material:
pp. 4-6, 11, 13, 16, 18, 19 Stephen J. Krasemann/DRK Photo; p. 7 Buddy Mays/Corbis; pp. 8, 15 John Cancalosi/DRK Photo; p. 9 Steve Kaufman/DRK Photo; p. 10 Joe McDonald/Corbis; pp. 12, 20, 24 Wayne Lynch/DRK Photo; p. 14 Anthony Mercieca/Photo Researchers, Inc.; p. 17 Mark Bowler/NHPA; p. 21 James Carmichael Jr./NHPA; p. 23 (t-b) Corbis, Corbis, Wayne Lynch/DRK Photo, Corbis; back cover (l-r) Corbis

Cover photograph by Joe McDonald/Corbis

50.64
J

Special thanks to our advisory panel for their help in the preparation of this book:

Alice Bethke
Library Consultant
Palo Alto, CA

Kathleen Gilbert
Second Grade Teacher
Round Rock, TX

Sandra Gilbert
Library Media Specialist
Fiest Elementary School
Houston, TX

Jan Gobeille, Kindergarten Teacher
Garfield Elementary
Oakland, CA

Angela Leeper
Educational Consultant
Wake Forest, NC

Pam McDonald
Reading Teacher
Winter Springs, FL

Contents

Some words are shown in bold, **like this.**
You can find them in the picture glossary on page 23.

Are Javelinas In Your Backyard?

It is not likely that you would see a javelina in your backyard.

Javelinas like to live in **forests**.

They hide in bushes and tall grass.

What Are Javelinas?

Javelinas are **mammals.**

Hair covers their bodies.

Javelinas are warm-blooded.

Their bodies make heat so they can stay warm wherever they are.

What Do Javelinas Look Like?

Javelinas have tube-shaped bodies.

They have short legs with **hooves**.

Javelinas have pointed heads and flat noses.

Their hair is gray, black and brown.

How Big
Are Javelinas?

Adult javelinas are as long as
a small bicycle.

They are as tall as a chair.

Small javelinas weigh as much as a small child.

Large javelinas weigh as much as two small children.

What Do Javelinas Feel Like?

hooves

Javelinas hair feels scratchy.

Their **hooves** are hard like fingernails.

Their noses feels soft and moist.

Javelinas tails feel like hairy string.

What Do Javelinas Eat?

Javelinas eat plants or animals.

They like bird and turtle eggs.

cactus

Javelinas eat roots and **cactus**.

They even eat dead animals.

What Is Something Special About Javelinas?

Javelinas have a very good sense of smell.

They can smell food buried in the ground.

Javelinas find things with their noses.

They dig food out with their **hooves**.

How Do Javelinas Stay Safe?

Javelinas try to stay away from danger.

They run away when scared.

Javelinas can run through bushes.

Bigger animals cannot follow.

Are Javelinas Dangerous To You?

Javelinas can be dangerous.

They can bite hard.

Javelinas try to stay away
from people.

But they will protect themselves or
their young.

Quiz

What are these javelina parts?

?

?

?

Picture Glossary

cactus
page 15
a prickly plant that usually grow in dry places

forest
page 5
a lot of trees and brushes covering a large area

hooves
page 8, 12, 17
a hard covering that protect the toes of the javelina

mammal
page 6
an animal that has fur or hair on its body and feeds its babies with milk from its body

Note to Parents and Teachers

Reading for information is an important part of a child's literacy development. Learning begins with a question about something. Help children think of themselves as investigators and researchers by encouraging their questions about the world around them. Each chapter in this book begins with a question. Read the question together. Look at the pictures. Talk about what you think the answer might be. Then read the text to find out if your predictions were correct. Think of other questions you could ask about the topic, and discuss where you might find the answers. Assist children in using the picture glossary and the index to practice new vocabulary and research skills.

! CAUTION: Remind children that it is not a good idea to handle wild animals. Children should wash their hands with soap and water after they touch any animal.

Index

Answers to quiz on page 22

tail

hooves

nose